Uniquely
Texas

Mary Dodson Wade

Heinemann Library
Chicago, Illinois

© 2004 Heinemann Library
a division of Reed Elsevier Inc.
Chicago, Illinois

Customer Service 888-454-2279

Visit our website at www.heinemannlibrary.com

Designed by Heinemann Library
Page layout by Patricia Stevenson
Printed and bound in the United States by
    Lake Book Manufacturing, Inc.

08 07 06 05 04
10 9 8 7 6 5 4 3 2 1

**Library of Congress
Cataloging-in-Publication Data**

Wade, Mary Dodson.
  Uniquely Texas / Mary Dodson Wade.
      p. cm. -- (Heinemann state studies)
Summary: Discusses the features that make Texas a
one-of-a-kind place,
including state government, state symbols, sports,
and cultural
features.
Includes bibliographical references and index.
  ISBN 1-4034-0691-X -- ISBN 1-4034-2699-6
  1. Texas--Juvenile literature. [1. Texas.] I. Title. II.
Series.
  F386.3.W36 2003
  976.4--dc21

2003009566

Acknowledgments

The author and publishers are grateful to the
following for permission to reproduce copyright
material:

Cover photography by (main) D. Boone/Corbis;
(top L-R) Dennis Flaherty/Photo Researchers, Inc.,
David R. Frazier Photolibrary, Jan Stromme/Bruce
Coleman Inc., Darrell Gulin/Corbis

Title page (L-R) James P. Rowan, Tom Bean/Corbis,
Steve Kaufman/Corbis; contents page Dennis
Flaherty/Photo Researchers, Inc.; p. 6 Scott
Berner/Visuals Unlimited; pp. 7, 37 David R. Frazier
Photolibrary; p. 8L Texas Secretary of State; p. 8R
Texas State Preservation Board; p. 11 Southern
Music Company; p. 12 Steve Kaufman/Corbis;
p.13T John Shaw/Bruce Coleman Inc.; pp. 13B,
19, 22, 33T Robert & Linda Mitchell; p. 14T
Dennis Flaherty/Photo Researchers, Inc.; p. 14B Joe
McDonald/Bruce Coleman Inc.; p. 15T Courtesy
www.puretexan.com; p. 15B Karen Carr; p. 16
Kelly-Mooney Photography/Corbis; pp. 17, 21 Bob
Daemmrich/The Image Works; p. 23 Dave G.
Houser/Corbis; p. 25 John Atashian/Corbis; p. 26
David Toase/PhotoDisc; p. 27 Steve Butman
Photography/Courtesy National Center for
Children's Illustrated Literature; p. 28 Jan
Stromme/Bruce Coleman Inc.; p. 29 AFP/Corbis;
pp. 30, 31T Joseph Sohm/ChromoSohm Inc./
Corbis; p. 31C Reuters NewMedia Inc./Corbis;
p. 31B Duomo/Corbis; p. 32 Noel Barnhurst/
FoodPix/Getty Images; p. 33B Mark Thomas/
FoodPix/Getty Images; p. 34 Chromosohm/Sohm/
Photo Researchers, Inc.; p. 35 James P. Rowan;
p. 38 Tom Bean/Corbis; p. 40T Texas Parks and
Wildlife; p. 40B Roger Ressmeyer/Corbis; p. 41
James P. Rowan; p. 42 Buddy Mays; p. 43 Michael
Burke/Index Stock Imagery; p. 44T Danny
Lehman/Corbis; p. 44B Pat Sullivan/AP Wide
World Photo

Photo research by Julie Laffin

Every effort has been made to contact copyright
holders of any material reproduced in this book.
Any omissions will be rectified in subsequent
printings if notice is given to the publisher.

Some words are shown in bold, **like this.**
You can find out what they mean by looking
in the glossary.

Contents

Texas Pride

Texans are proud of their state. Cars have bumper stickers that say "Native Texan." Even people who have moved to Texas from other places can buy ones that say "I wasn't born in Texas, but I got here as fast as I could." One of the reasons for Texas pride is that from 1836 to 1845 the state was its own nation. Texas became the 28th state of the United States in 1845.

BIG TEX

One thing Texans talk about is the state's size. Texas is big. Until Alaska became part of the United States, Texas was the largest state. With a total area of more

Unique Facts About Texas

1883—World's first rodeo held: Pecos

1885—Dr Pepper, a soft drink, invented by Charles Alderton: Waco

1900—Nation's worst natural disaster: hurricane causing 6,000 to 8,000 deaths in Galveston

1919—First play-by-play radio broadcast of a football game: University of Texas vs. Agricultural and Mechanical College of Texas in College Station

1938—World's largest medical center started: Texas Medical Center in Houston

1949—World's first round-the-world nonstop plane flight takes off and lands: Fort Worth

1952—World's largest rose garden started: Tyler Municipal Rose Garden, in Tyler

1965—Nation's first domed stadium built: the Astrodome, in Houston

1979—Nation's biggest rainfall in a 24-hour period: 43 inches in Alvin

Things to See in Texas

than 267,000 square miles, Texas is as large as Florida, Georgia, Alabama, Mississippi, Tennessee, and Massachusetts combined.

Texas also has the most people of any state in the country except California. The 2000 census showed nearly 21 million people living in Texas. Furthermore, Houston, Dallas, and San Antonio are three of the ten most populous cities in the United States. Harris County, where Houston is located, is the third most

Dressing Big Tex

Big Tex—all 52 feet of him—is how some people think a Texan should look. The statue has greeted visitors to the State Fair of Texas, in Dallas, for more than 50 years. He says, "Howdy, folks," and welcomes visitors in both English and Spanish. His size 70 boots may not be real, but his clothes are. Usually every other year he gets a new set. The weather is hard on his outfits. Lee, Wrangler, Williamson-Dickie, and other clothing companies have made his clothes. It takes 79 yards of material to make Big Tex's jeans. His last few outfits have been mostly red, white, and blue—the colors of the Texas flag.

populous county in the United States, with 3,400,578 people listed as residents. In addition, Texas has more miles of roads and highways and more miles of railroad track than any other state. It also has twice as many farms and more than twice as much farmland as any other state. The Port of Houston also ranks first in the United States in the amount of foreign goods that it handles.

Another unique feature of Texas is that it is the only state to have flown the flags of six different nations: Spain (1519–1685 and 1690–1821), France (1685–1690), Mexico (1821–1836), the **Republic** of Texas (1836–1845), the **Confederate** States (1861–1865), and the United States (1845–1861 and 1865–present). Read on to find out more unique and interesting things about Texas.

Texas State Symbols

LONE STAR FLAG

In 1839, the newly formed Republic of Texas adopted the Lone Star as its flag. The single white star on the blue background symbolizes Texas as an independent republic and is a reminder of the state's struggle for independence from Mexico. The flag's red color stands for bravery, white for purity, and blue for loyalty. Texas kept the same flag when it became part of the United States in 1845.

No one knows who designed the current flag. Some people think a person named Dr. Charles Stewart designed it. He

The Texas legislature mistakenly repealed the law that established the state flag in 1839. The legislature approved a new law in 1933 that reestablished the flag's design as official.

was on the committee that was appointed to produce a new state flag. The historical society in Montgomery, where Stewart lived for many years, has a copy of the design he drew. The second president of Texas, Mirabeau B. Lamar, approved the design in 1839.

TEXAS STATE SEAL

States use a seal to make documents official. One story says that the first Texans used a coat button as the state seal. The Texas government was so new that no seal existed. The story says that **provisional** Governor Henry Smith cut a button off his coat and pressed the button into wax. The design may have been a daisy. The state archives has papers with the seal, but the seal is not clear.

Reverse Sides of Seals

Both the United States and Texas have official reverse sides of their seals. The reverse of the Texas seal *(pictured right)* is used only as a decorative symbol. Unlike the front side *(pictured below)*, the reverse does not carry with it any legal use.

Governments found reverse sides useful when ribbons with wax pendants were used on documents. Officials pressed the reverse side into the wax along with the front side when sealing documents.

The Republic of Texas chose the official seal in 1836. Like the Lone Star, the Texas state seal has a five-pointed star. The oak branch on the left symbolizes strength, while the olive branch on the right stands for peace. Over the star were the words "The Republic of Texas." Texans changed the word *Republic* to *State* in 1845.

The reverse side of the Texas seal developed much later. It was adopted in 1961. It is based on a design by Sarah Farnsworth that was proposed by the Daughters of the Republic of Texas. It consists of a shield surrounded by the six national flags that have flown over Texas.

PLEDGE OF ALLEGIANCE TO THE TEXAS FLAG

In 1965, Governor John B. Connally signed the law making the pledge of allegiance to the Texas flag official. In some elementary schools, Texas children recite the pledge to the Texas flag right after the pledge to the U.S. flag. Texans also recite it at public meetings. The pledge honors the flag. It shows that Texans are united and proud of their state.

Honor the Texas flag;
I pledge allegiance to thee,
Texas, one and indivisible.

STATE MOTTO: FRIENDSHIP

Friendship was chosen as the state motto in 1930. But the idea for the motto goes back long before the Europeans came to present-day Texas in the 1500s. When the Spanish explorers arrived in what is now eastern Texas, they met the Caddo people. The Spaniards heard a Caddo word they understood to be *Tejas* (TAY-hahs). *Tejas* is the Caddo greeting, meaning "friends." Texas takes its name and motto from that word.

STATE NICKNAME: LONE STAR STATE

Texas is known as the Lone Star State. The nickname refers to the single star found on the state flag and state seal. The nickname also recalls the state's **heritage** as an independent country.

STATE SONG: "TEXAS, OUR TEXAS"

Texas's state song is called "Texas, Our Texas." William J. Marsh **copyrighted** the song in 1925. Marsh taught music at Texas Christian University, in Fort Worth. He composed the music and wrote the words with Gladys Yoakum Wright. "Texas, Our Texas" won a statewide contest sponsored by the Texas **legislature.**

In 1959, Texans had to make a slight change. In that year, Alaska joined the Union, and Texas was no longer the largest state. They changed the phrase "largest and grandest" in the first verse to "boldest and grandest."

"TEXAS, OUR TEXAS"

Texas, our Texas! All hail the mighty State!
Texas, our Texas! So wonderful, so great!
Boldest and grandest, Withstanding ev'ry test
O Empire wide and glorious, You stand supremely
  blest.

Chorus:
God bless you, Texas!
And keep you brave and strong,
That you may grow in power and worth,
Thro'out the ages long.

Texas, O Texas! Your freeborn Single Star,
Sends out its **radiance** to nations near and far.
Emblem of Freedom! It sets our hearts aglow,
With thoughts of San Jacinto and glorious Alamo.

"Texas, Our Texas" became the official state song in 1929.

Chorus:
> God bless you, Texas!
> And keep you brave and strong,
> That you may grow in power and worth,
> Thro'out the ages long.

> Texas, dear Texas! From tyrant grip now free,
> Shines forth in splendor your star of destiny!
> Mother of heroes! We come your children true,
> Proclaiming our allegiance, our faith, our Love
>> for You.

One famous mockingbird could reproduce 39 bird songs, 50 bird calls, and the sounds of a frog and a cricket.

STATE BIRD: MOCKINGBIRD

In 1927, the Texas Federation of Women's Clubs asked the **legislature** to choose a state bird. They chose the mockingbird, which is common in Texas. They are large birds—about ten inches long—with mostly gray feathers. The bird has an amazing ability to repeat sounds, even mechanical ones such as those of tractors. They get their name from their habit of imitating the calls of other birds.

STATE FLOWER: BLUEBONNET

In 1901, the legislature acted on a request from the Society of Colonial Dames in Texas to make the bluebonnet the state flower. Originally, they named only one kind of bluebonnet, not realizing there were many types of bluebonnets. The one named the state flower was not even the most common type in Texas. But Governor Preston Smith included other types of bluebonnets in 1971. He declared

The Texas Department of Transportation plants more than 33,000 pounds of wildflower seeds every year, including bluebonnet seeds.

that any of the varieties of bluebonnet qualified as the state flower.

STATE TREE: PECAN

Pecan trees grow tall, some more than 100 feet. The fruit of the pecan tree is the pecan nut—a sweet, **edible** nut. Texas is the country's second largest producer of pecans.

Governor James Hogg (1851–1906), the first **native** governor of Texas, loved pecan trees. He served as governor from 1891 to 1895. He asked that a pecan tree be planted at his grave. The Texas legislature made the pecan tree the official state tree in 1919 in Hogg's honor.

Only outsiders would dare pronounce pecan nuts "PEE-canz." In Texas, they are "puh-KAHNZ."

13

STATE LARGE MAMMAL: LONGHORN

In 1995, the Texas **legislature** named the longhorn, a particular breed of cattle, as the official state large **mammal.** More than ten million longhorns lived in the United States before the **Civil War** (1861–1865). Most were wild animals that could be claimed by anyone who could catch and brand them.

Longhorn horns, measured from tip to tip, span between two and eight feet.

However, in the early 1900s, more cattle breeds were introduced from Europe and Asia. Many of these animals were bred with the longhorn. This practice started the decline of the longhorn. By 1927, very few Texas longhorns remained. Thanks to recent efforts at saving them, more than a quarter million of them now live in Canada, Texas, and other states.

STATE REPTILE: HORNED LIZARD

Another state animal is the Texas horned lizard, the state reptile. Texans often call it a horned toad. It became the state reptile in 1993. The horned toad is a gentle creature. But it looks fierce

Adult horned lizards reach an average size of five inches. Horned lizards continually grow throughout their lives, though growth slows as they get older.

because its rough skin appears to have spikes. It is **threatened,** but not **endangered.** The law **prohibits** people from capturing horned toads.

In 1969, the legislature made Texas blue topaz the official state gem.

STATE GEM: BLUE TOPAZ

Texas is one of the few places in the world where you will find a blue topaz— a rare, pale blue stone. In Texas, the state **gem** is found only in the Llano Uplift, west of Mason.

STATE DINOSAUR: PLEUROCOELUS

Texas has a state dinosaur, the pleurocoelus (PLOOR-uh-SEEL-us). The legislature chose it in 1997. Pleurocoelus tracks can be found in the Paluxy River bed in Dinosaur Valley State Park. The pleurocoelus, as well as some other dinosaurs, made the tracks about 100 million years ago.

Pleurocoelus tracks range from 12 to 30 inches long and 9 to 24 inches wide.

STATE STONE: PETRIFIED PALMWOOD

The Texas legislature chose **petrified** palmwood, found mostly on the Texas Gulf Coast, as the state stone in 1969. Plants living 30 million years ago formed into the petrified palmwood found today.

Texas Government

Texas is still operating under its **constitution** adopted on February 15, 1876. A constitution is a plan for government. The Texas constitution has been amended, or changed, hundreds of times. The Texas constitution organizes state government into the same three branches as the federal government—**executive, legislative,** and **judicial.**

LEGISLATIVE BRANCH

The state legislative branch makes state laws. The Texas legislature is bicameral, which means it has two legislative houses. Like the U.S. government, Texas has a house of representatives and a senate.

In 2000 Austin, the Texas capital, had a population of more than 650,000 people.

Texas has 31 state senators and 150 state representatives. Representatives serve two-year **terms.** Senators serve four-year terms, but not all senators are up for reelection the same year.

This method makes sure that the senate always has some experienced **legislators.**

The Texas **legislature** meets in odd-numbered years. The sessions begin on the second Tuesday of January and last for 140 days. The governor can call a special session of the legislature. But he or she will do this only in an emergency, such as a major problem with the state **budget.** When the legislature is not in session, its members have other jobs, such as lawyers, doctors, and business owners.

For the legislature to add a new law, one or more legislators must sponsor a **bill.** A bill contains a proposal for a new law. Legislators then debate the positives and negatives of the bill. Both the house and the senate must approve the bill. If both houses approve a bill, the governor can still **veto** it. But the bill can still become law if enough legislators support the bill. They can **override** the governor's **veto.** It takes more votes to **override** a veto than to pass a **bill** the first time. If two-thirds of the **legislators** in both the house and senate vote to override a governor's veto, then the bill becomes a law.

The state uses a different method to amend its **constitution.** Legislators offer a resolution stating the change they want to make. A resolution is not a law. It simply says that the legislators approve of the idea. After two-thirds of the members of both houses approve the resolution, the amendment goes on the ballot for voters to approve. The governor cannot veto an amendment.

EXECUTIVE BRANCH

The **executive** branch of government carries out the state's laws. The governor is the head of the executive branch. Texas governors began serving four-year **terms** in 1975. A governor can be elected an unlimited number of times.

The Texas governor has much less power than most other state governors because she or he appoints only

Texas Railroad Commission

Texas has more miles of railroad track than any other state, but that is not what makes the Texas Railroad Commission so powerful. This office controls the amount of oil and natural gas that wells are allowed to produce. Oil and gas are important sources of money for the state. The state views pipelines as carriers, just like trains. That is why the state placed the Texas Railroad Commission in charge of oil and gas pipelines.

two state officials—the **secretary of state** and the **adjutant general.** As a result, much of the power in shaping the executive branch lies with the voters. They elect all other state offices. This gives voters a large amount of influence over the Texas executive branch when compared to most other states. Such positions as the **attorney general,** the **comptroller** of public accounts, and the **land commissioner** are not dependent on the governor for their jobs. These officials may not even be from the same political party as the governor.

JUDICIAL BRANCH

The **judicial** branch of government interprets the state's laws and decides how to apply them in real situations. These decisions are made in courts of law.

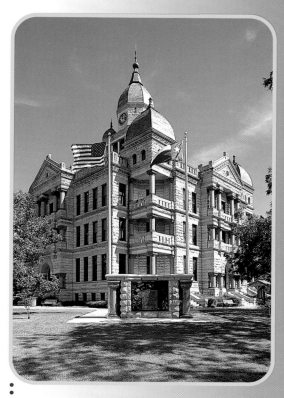

Many of Texas's old courthouses are still in use, including the one pictured above—the Denton County Courthouse (1896).

There are three general types of courts in Texas—trial, **appellate,** and final appellate courts. On the state level, trial courts include the district courts and **criminal** district courts. Trial courts on the local level include the municipal and justice of the peace (JP) courts. Trial courts have one judge. Evidence is presented and witnesses testify. If a jury hears a case, it will find the accused person either guilty or not guilty. Other cases are tried before a judge.

There are approximately 400 district courts in Texas. These courts are the general trial courts in Texas. Each county must be served by at least one district court. Several **rural** counties may have one district court, while

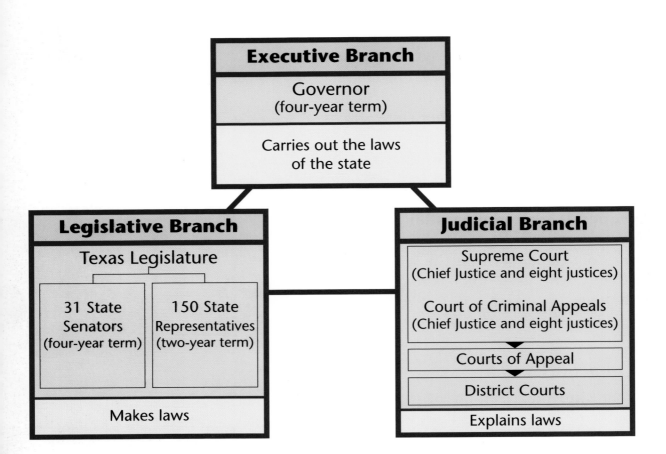

Executive Branch

Governor
(four-year term)

Carries out the laws
of the state

Legislative Branch

Texas Legislature

| 31 State Senators (four-year term) | 150 State Representatives (two-year term) |

Makes laws

Judicial Branch

Supreme Court
(Chief Justice and eight justices)

Court of Criminal Appeals
(Chief Justice and eight justices)

Courts of Appeal

District Courts

Explains laws

*Like the U.S. government, the Texas government is organized into three branches—the **legislative, executive,** and **judicial.***

an **urban** county may be served by many district courts. Examples of cases include **criminal** cases and divorce cases. Most district courts try both criminal and **civil** cases.

Approximately 850 cities and towns have **municipal** courts. Municipal courts try civil cases in which a person has violated a city ordinance, or law. Municipal judges can also issue search **warrants** to search a person's house. Larger Texas cities are served by many **municipal** courts. Every **incorporated** city or town in Texas has at least one municipal court.

JP courts are also trial courts at the municipal level of Texas government. There are about 900 JP courts in Texas.

Voting Machines

During the 2000 presidential election, many voters used paper ballots. They had to punch out holes to make their choices. In some cases, election officials had difficulty telling whether a voter had punched a particular hole. Because of problems counting paper ballot votes, Texas has begun to use electronic voting machines.

Each county has at least one JP court. JP courts try minor criminal cases, such as traffic and school attendance cases. A justice of the peace can perform marriages. She or he can also issue search or arrest **warrants.**

The next level of courts includes the fourteen courts of appeal. In an appeal, a person takes a decision from a lower court to a higher court for review. They hear both civil and criminal cases appealed from lower courts on the district or county level. Appeals are usually heard by a panel of three judges. The two sides present no new evidence and call no new witnesses. The question is whether the judge or jury in the lower court followed the law in reaching the decision.

The third level of courts include the highest courts in Texas—the Supreme Court of Texas and the Court of Criminal Appeals. These courts have the final say on the state level. Both courts have a presiding judge and eight other judges. The judges are elected for a six-year **term.**

The Texas Supreme Court handles only **civil** cases. For **criminal** cases, the highest state court is the Court of Criminal Appeals. Both the **prosecutor** and the **defendant** in criminal cases can file an appeal. In cases where a judge or jury has sentenced a person to death, that case is automatically appealed. The Court of Criminal Appeals has the final say in most criminal cases and in all cases involving the death penalty.

Old Courthouses

Many Texas courthouses are more than a century old. They are stone structures that look like fortresses or castles. Some towns have replaced the original buildings. But many, such as the ones in Denton, Marshall, and Waxahachie, are still in use. Following the Spanish idea of the plaza, courthouses often sit on large lawns squarely in the middle of a town. Traffic flows around them.

The oldest courthouse in Texas is called Old Cora. The 1856 log cabin is preserved in the town square in Comanche, northwest of Austin.

The Sherwood Courthouse in Irion County *(pictured above)*, which was built in 1901, belongs to the Sherwood Community Association because the county no longer needed the building. The county seat had moved to Mertzon, a couple of miles away, when the railroad went through there.

Presidents from Texas

GEORGE WALKER BUSH

George W. Bush (1946–) was an oil executive, part-owner of the Texas Rangers baseball club, and Texas governor before becoming the 43rd president of the United States in 2001. He won the presidency with fewer popular votes than his opponent. He, like his father George H. W. Bush, is a **Republican.**

GEORGE HERBERT WALKER BUSH

George H. W. Bush (1924–) came to Texas after graduating from Yale University. He was an oil executive before he became a member of Congress and then vice president. He became the 41st president of the United States in 1989.

LYNDON BAINES JOHNSON

Lyndon Baines Johnson (1908–1973) was born near Stonewall. After serving as a member of Congress and vice president, he was sworn in as the 36th president in 1963, following the **assassination** in Dallas of John F. Kennedy. Johnson was a **Democrat.**

Eisenhower was born in this house in Denison, Texas.

DWIGHT DAVID EISENHOWER

Dwight D. Eisenhower (1890–1969) was born in Denison, Texas. Shortly afterward, his family moved to Kansas. He became a general in the U.S. Army and in 1953 became the 34th president of the United States. He was a Republican.

Music and Culture

Texas has a wide variety of music and museums that produce a distinctive Texas **culture.**

TEXAS MUSIC

Two famous old songs about Texas are "Deep in the Heart of Texas" and "The Yellow Rose of Texas." "Yellow Rose" dates to the 1850s. During the **Civil War** (1861–1865), **Confederate** soldiers marched to its swinging rhythm. Then settlers and cowhands sang it.

Today, music in Texas ranges from country-western music to rock-and-roll and the blues. Several stars from Texas, including Tex Ritter and Jim Reeves, are members of the Country Music Hall of Fame. In addition, Clint Black, who is from Houston, and George Strait, who is from Pearsall, have made their names in country music. For example, Black has had ten albums that sold one million or more

"Home on the Range"

David W. Guion, a Texan, was a fine composer and musician trained in Europe. He hosted a New York City radio program in the 1920s. He also wrote and arranged songs. His best-known arrangement is the cowboy song "Home on the Range." A collection of his original scores and personal effects is at the International Festival-Institute in Round Top.

Clint Black's "Killin' Time" was named one of the 100 Greatest Songs of Country Music.

copies and has performed at halftime of the Super Bowl. Texan Buddy Holly, whose real name was Charles Hardin Holley, changed American music with his rock-and-roll singing style. His famous hits include "Peggy Sue." Sam Lightnin' Hopkins played the blues in places from eastern Texas to Paris, France. And Texan Lyle Lovett, who is from Klein, has won a Grammy Award, a music award.

Texas-born Dale Evans starred in Western movies, in which she sang with her husband, Roy Rogers. Willie Nelson, who was born in Abbott, Texas, sings a famous country-western tune called "Mama, Don't Let Your Babies Grow Up to Be Cowboys."

Cotton-Eyed Joe

A famous dance in Texas is the Cotton-Eyed Joe. This is a **line dance** in which everyone joins arms and snakes around the dance floor. No one knows why people call the dance Cotton-Eyed Joe.

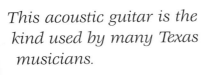

This acoustic guitar is the kind used by many Texas musicians.

Texas music features other string instruments besides the guitar. Dallas, Fort Worth, San Antonio, and Houston all have famous symphonies. For example, the Houston Symphony Orchestra is entering its 90th year.

The most surprising place to find both classical music and Shakespearean theater is in Winedale, a few miles from the tiny town of Round Top. Since 1971, the town of 87 residents has been the site of the International Festival-Institute. Students from all over the world come to study and perform summer concerts.

MUSEUMS

Museums and **cultural** centers around Texas hold collections of art from many different periods. For example, the University of Texas at Austin has a collection of rare books. It has one of five copies in the United States of the Gutenberg Bible, which was printed between 1454 and 1455.

Van Cliburn

Van Cliburn, a **native** Texan, surprised the music world by winning the first International Tchaikovsky Piano Competition in Moscow in 1958. The competition took place during the Cold War (1945–1991). The Cold War was a time of tension between the United States and the Soviet Union, most of which is now known as Russia. Cliburn was warmly received there. Although the judges expected a Soviet to win, Cliburn played better. In honor of his surprise win, a group of Fort Worth music teachers and volunteers started the Van Cliburn International Piano Competition. It is held in Fort Worth every four years.

Henkel Square is a museum village in the center of Round Top. It includes pioneer German buildings and decorative arts. Just a few miles away is the Winedale Historical Center. It was a gift to the University of Texas from Ima Hogg, a Houston art **patron.** Winedale also has a collection of early Texas houses from the 1800s. In addition, each summer in Winedale students give performances of plays by the great English playwright William Shakespeare.

The National Center for Children's Illustrated Literature, in Abilene, is a unique Texas museum. As the brainchild of Abilene mayor Gary McCaleb, the center opened as a place where art from children's illustrated literature would be honored. Many of the center's exhibits tour the United States.

On September 14, 2000, the National Center for Children's Illustrated Literature opened to the public.

Texas Sports

Texas loves sports. It especially loves rodeo and football.

RODEO

In professional rodeos, bronc riders and bulldoggers earn money. A bronc, or bronco, is a rodeo horse that bucks while the rider tries to stay on. Bulldogging is another name for steer wrestling. In that event, the cowboy leaps off his horse, grabs the bull by the horns, and wrestles it to the ground. The cowboys compete for points that lead to a national championship. **Amateurs** compete in local events. The Texas Cowboy Reunion, in Stamford, began in 1930. It is held each year during the three days that include the Fourth of July. The Stamford rodeo draws 500 contestants. It is the largest amateur rodeo in the world.

During a rodeo, a rider must stay on a bucking bronco for a set time—usually eight seconds.

SPORTS MANIA

High school football is a Friday night **tradition** in Texas. Football began in Texas in 1892, though championships did not become official until 1920. Sometimes entire towns, such as Celina, Texas—with a population of about

The First Rodeo

Rodeo is probably the state's oldest sport. Rodeos give ranch hands a chance to show off their skills, some of which include lassoing calves and horseback riding. The town of Pecos, Texas, organized a rodeo in 1883. Residents there claim it was the first rodeo in the world. The Texas Rodeo Hall of Fame is also in Pecos.

2,000—shut down to watch their team play. From 1998 to 2001, the people of Celina watched their team win four straight high school championships in its division and set a Texas high school record by winning 68 straight games.

Large universities such as Texas A&M University and the University of Texas at Austin have stadiums that hold more than 80,000 fans. The University of Texas at Austin has won three national collegiate football championships, while Texas A&M has one. Since 1917, the teams have combined for 46 conference championships.

The Dallas Cowboys, of the National Football League (NFL), play at Texas Stadium in Irving. The Cowboys have gone to the Super Bowl eight times and have won five times. Such all-time greats as Roger Staubach and Tony Dorsett led the Cowboys to two Super Bowl wins in

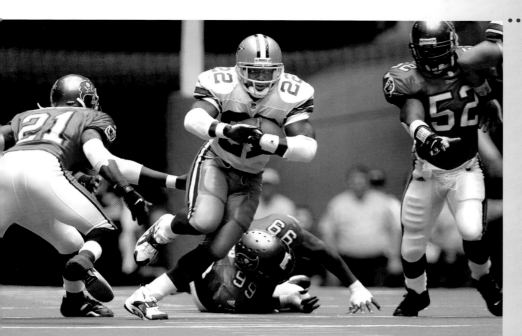

Longtime Dallas Cowboy Emmitt Smith, the NFL's career rushing leader, runs for daylight against the Tampa Bay defense.

the 1970s, while Troy Aikman and Emmitt Smith led the Cowboys to three straight Super Bowl titles in the 1990s. In 2002, a new NFL team, the Houston Texans, played their first game in Reliant Stadium.

BASEBALL, BASKETBALL, AND HOCKEY

The Houston Astros have a new baseball stadium on the edge of downtown called Minute Maid Park. Near Dallas, the Texas Rangers built a traditional open-air stadium. It is called The Ballpark in Arlington.

Astrodome

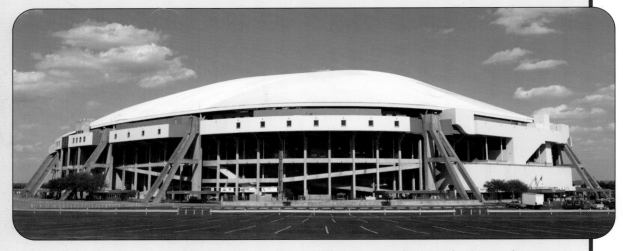

In Houston, Harris County built the first fully air-conditioned, domed sports stadium. The Astrodome served many different sports. The building opened with a Houston Astros baseball game in 1965. For years, fans watched football games, baseball, rodeos, monster-truck events, and motocross races in the stadium's constant 73°F temperature. In October 1999, almost 50,000 people watched the Atlanta Braves win the last game ever played at the Astrodome. The Astrodome is still open, but it is used for nonsporting events.

Texas Ranger Alex Rodriguez high-fives a teammate after a home run at The Ballpark in Arlington.

Texas has three National Basketball Association (NBA) teams. The San Antonio Spurs, led by David Robinson and Tim Duncan, won the NBA championship in 1999 and 2003. In addition, the Houston Rockets, led by Hakeem Olajuwon, won the championship for two straight years, in 1994 and 1995. The Dallas Mavericks made it to the conference finals in 2003. When the NBA formed the Women's National Basketball Association (WNBA), the Houston Comets took the first four titles, from 1997 to 2000.

In 1993, the National Hockey League's (NHL) Minnesota North Stars moved south and became the Dallas Stars. The Stars have achieved great success, winning the NHL's Stanley Cup Championship in 1999 and making it to the Stanley Cup Finals in 2000.

Houston Comet Sheryl Swoopes dribbles the basketball in a game against the New York Liberty.

Texas Food

Texans love spicy food, and one of their favorite dishes is chili. They also love desserts, especially ones made with the state nut—the pecan.

TEXAS CHILI

Chili is one of the most popular dishes in Texas. Most Texans agree that real Texas chili does not have any beans, just meat and an array of spices and peppers. Cooks have their favorite meat—**venison,** squirrel, or rattlesnake. Some recipes include onions, tomatoes, garlic, or other ingredients the cook likes. But cooks

The mixture of meat, beans, peppers, and spices known to Texans as chili was also made hundreds of years earlier by the Incas, Aztecs, and Mayans— cultures that lived in present-day Latin America.

Texas cooks use all kinds of peppers—hot, mild, green, red, dried, or fresh.

must grind these ingredients so finely that people cannot see them. Some people keep their recipes a secret and claim to put something special in the chili. A man once said that he threw in an old boot!

PECAN PIE

A favorite Texan dessert—pecan pie—has many different versions, such as chocolate. But try the recipe below for a traditional version.

Pecan Pie Recipe

Mix together:
- 1 cup light brown sugar
- 1 tablespoon butter, softened
- 1 heaping tablespoon flour
- dash salt

Add one at a time:
- 3 eggs, beaten
- 1 cup white corn syrup
- 1 teaspoon vanilla
- 1 cup broken pecans

Place in uncooked 9" pie shell.

Have an adult help you. Bake at 300°F for 50–60 minutes, or until center does not shake when pie plate is moved.

Monuments to Texas History

Texans are proud of their history, and the state is filled with many historic buildings and monuments.

The Texas capitol is taller than the U.S. capitol. When it was finished in 1888, it had 392 rooms, 924 windows, and 404 doors.

THE TEXAS CAPITOL

Texans built the current capitol building to match the size of their state—big. The design is similar to the Capitol in Washington, D.C., but the Texas capitol is taller. It rises 311 feet from the ground to the top of the

statue on the dome. The capitol's outside walls are made from Texas red granite, while the interior and dome walls are Texas limestone. It took six years to finish the building. A fifteen-and-one-half-foot statue called the *Goddess of Liberty* stands on the dome. The original 2,050-pound zinc *Goddess of Liberty* had stood on the dome for 98 years. The state replaced the statue with an identical one made of aluminum. The original *Goddess of Liberty* is now in the Texas State History Museum, in Austin. The reverse of the state seal is on the floor of the underground **rotunda.** The building was designated a National Historic Landmark in 1986.

THE ALAMO

The Spanish established several **missions** in central Texas in the late 1600s and early 1700s. One of these—Mission San Antonio de Valero, which later became known as the Alamo—was established between 1716 and 1718. *Alamo* is Spanish for "cottonwood tree." The Alamo became famous during the Texas Revolution, which began in 1835. In December 1835, a small number of Texas soldiers occupied the Alamo, located in central San Antonio.

The restored chapel and grounds of the Alamo honor the Texans who died defending the Alamo during the Texas Revolution.

The Republic of Texas

In the mid-1830s, the Mexican government began to assert its control over Texas, then part of Mexico. Many American settlers, which numbered close to 30,000 by 1836, were not following Mexican laws. For example, Mexico did not allow slavery, but settlers in Texas still brought in slaves. The Mexican government wanted to maintain control in their own country, while the settlers saw themselves as living under a **tyrannical** government. During the Texas Revolution (1835–1836), in which the settlers defeated Mexico, the Republic of Texas was established. In 1836, Sam Houston became Texas's first president, and Stephen F. Austin became its first secretary of state. Cities were named in their honor—Houston was the capital from 1837 until 1839. Austin was approved as the permanent capital in 1850. The republic had a hard ten-year life. It had no money, and raiding Native Americans and Mexicans threatened its people. Texas finally joined the United States on December 29, 1845.

Texas leaders such as Sam Houston thought that San Antonio would be impossible to defend with the small number of troops. However, the volunteers at the Alamo refused to leave their position. On February 23, 1836, a Mexican army of about 4,000 soldiers laid **siege** to the Alamo. The small Texan force of about 189 soldiers held out for 13 days. But on the morning of March 6 the Mexicans finally overwhelmed the Texans. Only about a few people, mostly women and children, survived. The Mexicans suffered heavy casualties, with almost 1,600 dead. These casualties and the time lost in taking the Alamo hurt the Mexican campaign and allowed Texas leader Sam Houston to perfect plans for the defense of Texas.

SAN JACINTO MONUMENT

Another monument to the Texas Revolution is in La Porte, twenty miles southeast of Houston. The San Jacinto Battleground State Historic Site is where Texas general Sam Houston's army defeated the troops of Mexican general Santa Anna and captured Santa Anna himself. On April 21, 1836, the small Texas force of 900 men surprised the Mexican army, which numbered about 1,300. The battle lasted less than 30 minutes. During the fighting, the Texans killed, wounded, or captured the entire Mexican force. This victory led to Texas's independence from Mexico.

When the San Jacinto Monument was completed, it was the highest concrete structure in the world. The 567-foot shaft looks like the Washington Monument. The face is made of limestone that contains **fossils.** The limestone was taken from a **quarry** near Austin.

Completed in 1939, the San Jacinto Monument was built more than twelve feet higher than the Washington Monument.

Attractions
and
Landmarks

Texas's national and state parks offer everyone a wide variety of activities. Texas's cities have many cultural attractions, too.

BIG BEND

Big Bend National Park covers over 801,000 acres of west Texas in the place where the Rio Grande makes a sharp turn—the Big Bend. It is the eighth-largest national park in the continental United States. It was established on June 12, 1944, and designated a U.S. Biosphere Reserve in 1976. Big

The vast Boquillas Canyon cuts through Big Bend National Park.

Texas State and National Parks

Legend:
- 🌲 State/Regional Park
- National Park

Amarillo
Palo Duro Canyon
Caprock Canyons
Copper Breaks
Lake Arrowhead
Eisenhower
Bonham
Atlanta
Fort Richardson & Lost Creek Reservoir
Lake Bob Sandlin
Daingerfield
Fort Griffin
Possum Kingdom
Fort Worth
Dallas
Caddo Lake
Lake Colorado City
Cedar Hill
Sabine River
Tyler
Big Spring
Abilene
Purtis Creek
Tyler
Martin Creek Lake
Midland
Abilene
Dinosaur Valley
Rusk/Palestine
San Angelo
Meridian
Fairfield Lake
Caddoan Mounds
Colorado
Waco
Mission Tejas
Pecos
Mother Neff
Confederate Reunion Grounds
Fort McKavett
Colorado Bend
Fort Boggy
Balmorhea
Fort Lancaster
Enchanted Rock
Longhorn Cavern
Huntsville
Lake Livingston
Davis Mountains
South Llano River
Pedernales Falls
Blanco
Guadalupe River
Austin
McKinney Falls
Beaumont
Devils River
Village Creek
Fort Leaton
Seminole Canyon
Honey Creek
Buescher
Stephen F. Austin
Big Bend Ranch
Big Bend National Park
Devil's Sinkhole
Hill Country
Brazos Bend
Houston
Sea Rim
Kickapoo Cavern
Palmetto
San Antonio
Galveston Island
Lost Maples
Rio Grande
Choke Canyon
Goliad
Fannin Battleground
Goose Island
Matagorda Island
Lake Corpus Christi
Lake Casa Blanca International
Mustang Island
Corpus Christi
Laredo
Gulf of Mexico
Falcon
Bentsen-Rio Grande Valley
Boca Chica

Franklin Mountains
Hueco Tanks
El Paso
Guadalupe Mountains National Park

0   100 mi.

Bend is famous for its variety of **species.** The park boasts more types of birds, bats, and cacti than any other national park in the country.

Some of Texas's more than 125 state parks and historic sites are shown here.

BIG THICKET NATIONAL PRESERVE

Big Thicket's 97,000 acres became the first preserve in the National Park system on October 11, 1974. Located near Beaumont, this area is unique because during the last **ice age,** eastern hardwood forests, the Gulf coastal plains, and the Midwest prairies were brought together in one geographical location. On December 15, 1981, the preserve was designated an International Biosphere Reserve by the United Nations Education, Scientific and Cultural Organization (UNESCO).

Submerged Pictographs

Amistad Dam was built on the Rio Grande to provide flood control as well as to provide water for farmers in dry southern Texas. When the reservoir filled, water backed up into the Pecos River for fourteen miles and into Devils River almost that far. Prehistoric people had made their homes in rock shelters along the river thousands of years ago. They  left pictographs that were protected by the overhanging ledges. The Amistad Reservoir flooded hundreds of the rock shelters. But artists made copies of as many as they could before water covered the pictographs. People can reach Panther Cave, named for the pictograph of the large, leaping panther in it, only by boat.

STONE AGE ARTIFACTS

People have been living in Texas for approximately 11,000 years. Some of the oldest **pictographs** in the Americas are in the Lower Pecos River area. Seminole Canyon State Park and Historic Site, near Del Rio, has pictographs that are between 4,000 and 6,000 years old. The pictographs are of animals, humans, graceful stick figures, and geometric designs. More modern pictures represent **mission** churches, Spanish explorers, and U.S. soldiers.

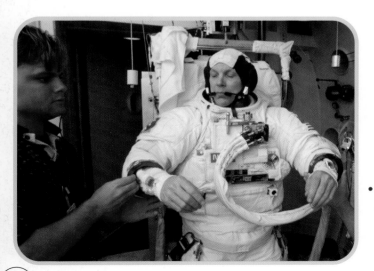

JOHNSON SPACE CENTER

In 1969, astronaut Neil Armstrong spoke from the moon, saying, "Houston...the *Eagle* has landed." A year later, Apollo Thirteen commander

An astronaut prepares for mission simulation at the Johnson Space Center.

James Lovell sent an alarming message from space: "Houston, we have a problem." Astronauts say "Houston," but they are really talking to people at the Johnson Space Center, in Clear Lake, twenty miles southeast of Houston. This is where the control center for the National Aeronautic and Space Administration (NASA) is located. Fifteen thousand engineers, scientists, and astronauts work and train at the Johnson Space Center. The center is named for Texan Lyndon Baines Johnson, the 36th president of the United States. Next door, visitors to Space Center Houston can walk around rockets, learn how astronauts live in space, and try landing an 85-ton spaceship using a computer simulator.

Military Heritage in Texas

The USS *Texas* was an important ship and claims many U.S. Navy firsts. In 1916, it became the first U.S. battleship to have antiaircraft guns and the first to control its

The USS Texas *served the U.S. Navy from 1914 to 1948.*

Flying off the USS Texas

Several experiments aboard the *Texas* helped improve the navy. For instance, in 1919 a pilot flew a Sopwith Camel, a World War I (1914–1918) warplane, off the deck of the *Texas*. This flight led to the development of aircraft carriers, which are perhaps the most important ships in the U.S. Navy today.

guns with directors and range-keepers, the forerunners of today's computers. In 1939, it received the first radar in the U.S. Navy. On April 21, 1948, the navy took the USS *Texas* out of service. It became the first battleship memorial museum in the country and is now a National Historic Landmark. The *Texas* is anchored on the Houston Ship Channel.

The world's only flying B-29 Superfortress is Fifi, *which belongs to the Commemorative Air Force (CAF).*

The Texas Commemorative Air Force (CAF) is a group of volunteers that preserves models of all U.S. and some foreign military aircraft from World War II (1939–1945). Its origins date to 1957. The volunteers fly the planes at air shows. The CAF museum and international headquarters are at the Midland International Airport. The CAF operates the only flying examples of the B-29 Superfortress and a German Heinkel He-111 bomber.

THE SAN ANTONIO RIVER WALK

During the first half of the 1900s, San Antonio's River Walk emerged. On March 14, 1941, a carnival and night parade were held on the San Antonio River. In addition, the walkways, stairways to street level, rock walls lining the banks, and the Arneson River Theatre were completed. Since that time, the River Walk has grown into Texas's most popular tourist attraction. Visitors can enjoy shopping, a dinner boat ride, or they can even get married! The River Walk is considered a city park and is maintained and operated by the City of San Antonio.

Texans and visitors alike enjoy strolling the River Walk during Christmastime.

This replica in the LBJ Library shows the Oval Office as it looked during Johnson's time as president.

PRESIDENTIAL LIBRARIES

Located at the University of Texas at Austin is the Lyndon Baines Johnson Library. It contains more than 40 million papers dealing with events during President Johnson's time in office, from 1963 to 1969. His **term** saw some of the most important events in U.S. history, including the Vietnam War (1955–1975) and the Civil Rights movement (1950s–1968). Among the permanent exhibits are Johnson's 1968 Lincoln limousine.

Located at Texas A&M University in College Station is the George H.W. Bush Presidential Library and Museum. It features exhibits on events during Bush's time in office, from 1989 to 1993. His term took place during some of the most important events in the second half of the 1900s, including the reunification of Germany (1990) and the collapse of the Soviet Union (1991).

George H.W. Bush is joined by then President Bill Clinton and former presidents Gerald Ford and Jimmy Carter on the stage at the Bush Library dedication in 1997.

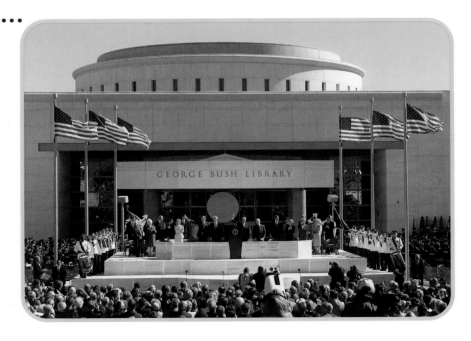

Map of Texas

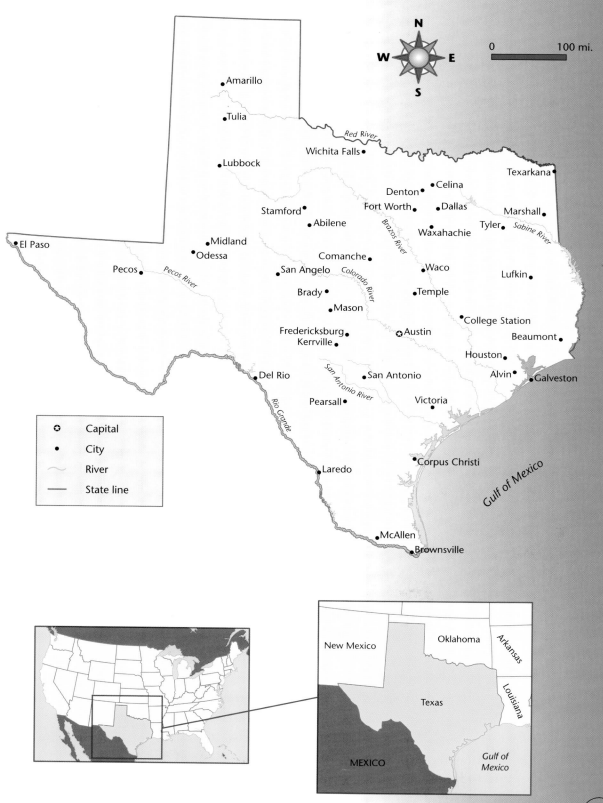

Legend:
- ✪ Capital
- • City
- ～ River
- — State line

Cities and features shown on the map:

Amarillo, Tulia, Lubbock, Wichita Falls, Texarkana, Denton, Celina, Fort Worth, Dallas, Marshall, Stamford, Abilene, Waxahachie, Tyler, Midland, El Paso, Odessa, Comanche, Waco, Lufkin, Pecos, San Angelo, Brady, Temple, Mason, College Station, Fredericksburg, Kerrville, Austin, Beaumont, Houston, Del Rio, San Antonio, Alvin, Galveston, Pearsall, Victoria, Laredo, Corpus Christi, McAllen, Brownsville

Red River, Brazos River, Sabine River, Pecos River, Colorado River, Rio Grande, San Antonio River, Gulf of Mexico

Inset map: New Mexico, Oklahoma, Arkansas, Texas, Louisiana, MEXICO, Gulf of Mexico

Glossary

adjutant general official who oversees the military department of the state

amateur a person who takes part in something for pleasure and not for pay

appellate a court that reviews decisions made by lower courts

assassination murder

attorney general chief law officer of a nation or state

bill proposed law presented to the legislature for approval

budget a plan for using money

Civil War the war between the Northern and Southern states of the United States from 1861 to 1865

comptroller official who controls the collecting and spending of money for the state

Confederate relating to the Confederacy, or the Southern states, during the **Civil War**

constitution plan for government

copyright get the exclusive right to publish or sell an artistic work

criminal having to do with a crime

culture ideas, skills, arts, and way of life of a certain people at a certain time

defendant person accused of a crime in a court of law

Democrat member of the Democratic Party

edible safe to eat

emancipation freedom

endangered in danger of dying off

executive branch of government that makes sure laws are carried out

fossil the remains of an ancient plant or animal. Most fossils are remains that have turned to stone or whose outlines have been preserved in stone.

gem a high-quality stone that is made into jewelry

heritage something that comes from one's ancestors

ice age period of colder climate when thick sheets of ice cover large regions of Earth. The last ice age ended about 11,500 years ago.

incorporated a specific type of government for a city or town

judicial branch of government that explains laws. It includes the courts.

land commissioner official who oversees public lands in a state

legislative branch of government that makes laws

legislature governmental body that makes and changes laws. A legislator is a lawmaker.

line dance type of dance in which dancers are in a line

mammal class of animals covered with hair (or fur or wool) that feed milk to their young

mission buildings made by the Spanish to protect Spanish territory and spread the Catholic religion

municipal having to do with a city or town

native belonging to a particular place by birth

override to overrule a decision

patron supporter

petrified turned into stone

pictograph ancient painting on rock

prosecutor lawyer in charge of the side of a case against an accused person

provisional temporary

quarry rock mine

radiance glow

republic a nation or state in which the people elect representatives to run the government

Republican member of the Republican Party

rotunda a round room with a high ceiling

rural relating to the countryside

secretary of state official responsible for keeping state records

siege a blockade of a place to force it to surrender

species a certain related group of animals

term set period of time

threatened likely to become in danger of dying off

tradition custom or belief handed down from generation to generation

tyrannical ruling with absolute authority in an oppressive or brutal way

urban relating to the city

venison deer meat

veto forbid or prevent

warrant an official order to do something

More Books to Read

· ·

Bredeson, Carmen. *Texas.* Tarrytown, N.Y.: Marshall Cavendish, 1997.

Hanson-Harding, Alexandra. *Texas.* Danbury, Conn.: Children's Press, 2001.

Heinrichs, Ann. *Texas.* Danbury, Conn.: Children's Press, 1999.

Sievert, Teri. *Texas.* Mankato, Minn.: Capstone, 2003.

Index

About the Author

Mary Dodson Wade spent 25 years as an elementary school librarian. Now, she writes full-time and has more than 40 books in print, with more to come. She lives in Houston and loves to write about her favorite state. Wade has also traveled all over the world with her husband.